Swimming with Jellyfish
Stuart Pickford

smith|doorstop

Published 2016 by
smith|doorstop books
The Poetry Business
Bank Street Arts
32-40 Bank Street
Sheffield S1 2DS
www.poetrybusiness.co.uk

Copyright © Stuart Pickford 2016

ISBN 978-1-910367-59-9

British Library Cataloguing-in-Publication Data.
A catalogue record for this book is available from the
British Library.

Typeset by Utter
Printed and bound by CPI Group (UK) Ltd, Croydon, CR0 4YY
Cover image: Wading Boy by Matthew Davis
Author photo: Stuart Pickford

smith|doorstop is a member of Inpress,
www.inpressbooks.co.uk. Distributed by Central Books Ltd.,
99 Wallis Road, London E9 5LN.

The Poetry Business receives financial support from
Arts Council England

Supported by
ARTS COUNCIL
ENGLAND

Contents

Storywaters

For Jan

Skin

Growing older is lying in bed
when a child, feeling the world
on your skin, opening your eyes to
the colour of your favourite toys
and thinking it is all still here.
Maybe you look up at how
leaves understand sun as shade,
maybe you wonder about the orbit
your life's on and what it's circling
but come Friday the beer tastes good
and you're ticklish under your chin.
There's the body. You're tattooed
with scars, the skin's loosening
and grey hairs aren't really blond.
But you can still outrun the stream
spluttering down the valley,
its trees lifted onto tiptoe
by wind. Your heart purrs,
lungs absorb pockets of sunlight,
blood warms each finger
till you sweat like a dog. Nothing
as simple as outside and in.
The mind's cool and smiles
at this simultaneous song
your skin sings.

The Lost Runner

In backs of cars, children's heads turn.
He doesn't break sweat crossing the park,
flits across CCTV passing SPAR,
laps up the bypass mapping the stars.

He grows solid out of a blur of mist,
past the first toddler on the swings,
clocked by smokers outside a pub,
overtaken by the last flickering train.

That's him – clues in fresh snow,
slaloming clumps of daffodils, leaning
into the rain. He cuts the heat haze
like water, running down the days.

Sinew in lycra, high-vis vest,
he sprints through Lingerie in the store,
jogs the reference section of the library,
leaves his footprints along the shore.

Is his body hydraulic, his blood digital?
What's coiled inside his heart?
What throws him out on a pig of a night,
endorphins telling him it doesn't hurt?

Shortest Day

I run along the beach. Sea
lays out the dying light.
Two kids write their names
in sand. The tide tips
from one thing to the next.

I run back. Each black wave
is trumped by another. I jump
the lovers' heart, keep on.
Out there, fathoms fill
with a lone humpback's song.

Moon

For Show and Tell, Jack's doing
Native American moons. We exhaust
the internet, then tog up to look at it,
me wondering why I wasn't surprised
the moon was once part of the earth.

Tonight it's not the strawberry moon
but the wolf. Through binoculars
there's its skull, the line of the snout,
the grey eye socket. In the dark
its cry would appear like our white breath.

*Another American story of the moon
is Apollo's,* I say: Buzz Aldrin,
Stars and Stripes stuck in the dust,
bunny-hopping footprints, lost
golf balls in the Sea of Tranquility.

Jack focuses the binoculars, listens
to how Michael Collins remained alone
on the mother ship that slipped behind
the dark side of the moon, the furthest
anyone had ever been from Earth.

We imagine the radio static. One
of our stories will be the two of us:
the dead rock locked in its orbit,
its light crossing the ice to reach us,
Jack pressing in against the cold.

Duchy Grove

I lead God by the hand to meet my street.
There, I say, is the quiet couple on the end
with their quiet son and daughter in the attic.
When we snapped their aerial playing night cricket
and took round the cheque, they said, *Thank you.*
Here's Mark, the screen printer, who's thrown money
at his place till it's a picture, framed. His back yard,
a herb garden. Next door, Fiona's wisteria
is a vine. Divine. And that was Nick, thighs
to the neck, focused on a 10k PB,
tracked by his satellite watch. Number 4,
Rita Jones. She'll be loving her neighbour
as I speak, blinds dropped all afternoon.
You know the rest. Wigsy is the white van.
If heaven needs sanding, he's your man.
Next door, the spy from Menwith Hill:
a southern drawl, novel or three in Russian,
Polish girlfriend, ear or two to the wall.
He knows who the Pope tweets but if he told you...
Our house? In the middle of the street. It's madness.
God smiled—he'd heard it, could hum the tune
as each window blared a different song.
Twice he'd tripped on roller blades in the yard.
Evening, smoke from barbies breezing through
jumping socks and vests and G-strings, bats
going crazy about the straight road, the hiss of tinnies.
Elbow on coalbunker, God said, *Chuck us a cold one.*
Downing his third, I was about to ask him
why two sooty terraces mirroring each other
is called a grove, but his face had an expression
that passed all understanding. I knew the answer.

Lighthouse

From the moment we cruise into
the disabled spot with sea views
right outside the Visitor Centre,
the day has our name on it.

Here, as boys, my brother and I
would gaze at the tiny ferries
while chewing our Marmite sandwiches
and wonder where *abroad* began.

Dad takes me aside for a word
about your mother overdoing it
and we're away across the Downs,
Mum waving her stick athletically.

There are *blue skies over* and butterflies,
more butterflies than I can remember,
peacocks, ones speckled like tobacco;
the heads of the flowers are floating.

We rest above the Scallop Shell,
the landslip, and chat about Christmas
when Mum spots a yellow bird
we'll look up later at home.

At the lighthouse, the guide laments
how it's now obsolete – all shipping
has sat nav – but the captains
still look up to know it's there.

The cliff leads us down to the bay.
Dad's driven the car around
and waited. There, there he is
sitting outside the pub, waving.

Scrumping

A week after your stroke,
you take my arm. Our plan:
the cherry plum tree.

My accomplice, you hold the bag.
From branches fit for the fire,
I reach for a hundred suns.

Your dad used to come here
as a boy. Like him, I leave
fingerprints on their waxy skins.

The bag grows fat. We discuss
marmalades, conserves, crumbles,
flans – nothing is impossible.

Across the lane, evening
lays shadows into which we
disappear, villains from a film.

We check sell-by dates,
a crumpled bag of sugar.
One withered lemon.

The golden flesh splutters,
plops into plastic tubs.
The freezer spikes with ice.

In hours, not jam, not
summer preserved for winter,
but the taste of now.

We've magicked our own sorbet
from the constellation of plums.
Its tang thaws on our tongues.

Sugar-stealers

Those globes of air.

I asked about their name.
You always find them
snagged in sugar bowls.

Dad cuts the lawn,
lays down rows, stops
for every bee on clover.

Mum folds washing –
takes it easy after her stroke.
A sugar-stealer idles in.

She catches it like
a butterfly. *In the wash,*
they end up as grey lumps.

She carries the sugar-stealer
in the locket of her hands,
a star of the day.

The mower powers down.
Good, Dad says, *I'll keep that*
for later and eases it
into his top pocket.

Dads at Weddings

What is it about poems with dads at weddings?
Suits fashionable second time around,
they kiss all the bone-china aunts
and wink, *Cruising for a toy boy, Gladys?*

Shaking hands, they imperceptibly nod
Fred with an eloquence that says I'm sorry
about your little scare: the asbestos factory,
dust falling on windowsills like snow.

Ruffling the hair of nippers, the dads
chuck them above their heads and spin them
like plates in Saturday-night game shows
or point to their chests, *What's there, Cocker?*

In all versions of the story, the dads run
fingers right up to their toothy grins.
Always a fiver from the wad of readies
in their back pockets for being good.

They scrub up well, their shirts one size
too small but their cufflinks, they're real gold.
Never complaining, the dads crack out
their limbs – crooners on a come-back tour.

An hour later, ties undone, pints in hand,
they're not throwing a few shapes in the marquee.
They face fat Uncle Billy and waddle in to the beat
like penguins, bouncing off each other's bellies.

Midnight, the dads are on the Bacardi. Everyone
has met them. In my poem, they're the last
to leave, jackets flung over their shoulders,
swaying, perhaps their other arm around you.

What's Wrong with David?

David does the garden. Ever since the ramp,
I've been keeping an eye, sometimes
he says to me the grass is too short
or too wet to be cut. To be fair,

till now he's been the bees' knees, as I have,
finding him jobs to do in winter: the leaves,
stuff in the greenhouse. He always has a coffee,
chocolate biscuits and a chat—at Margaret's

he gets bugger all, works straight through.
Pay-wise, cash in hand, always a quid
above the going rate. But last Tuesday,
he turns his nose up at the lawn. Himself

wants to trim the heather. Now I know
he's dapper with his cropped Tom Jones beard
but it's still in bloom. I wheel myself
round to the mower in the shed. Your David's

got the blade at the middle setting, no good
for this time of year when it grows a foot
a week. And when he does cut it, he walks
too quick, just combing it flat. No wonder

there's couch grass and all sorts coming through.
I'm not having Margaret's looking plush
while mine looks shithouse. It might be his teeth,
all those front ones, they're not his own.

24-Hour Care

Gone nine and he's drooping.
Mum and I prop him up in the chair.
I kneel before him to drag
his anti-slip Fire Socks over fat ankles.
He's in Mum's fleecy trackie bottoms
with the white stripe down the side
and a red star on the thigh, the ones
he hates her wearing. 73 years old.
The University of Virginia.

She feeds the drip down his sleeve,
drapes the dressing gown over his paunch.
I stuff the inflatable neck pillow
under his chin like a bib. She clicks
into place the false teeth I'll find
at 4 on the floor. Sleep tight, Dad.

I turn to Mum to take her arm
but her eyes are smouldering.
Grey cells start to drop
from her fingertips onto the carpet.
I look through where she stood
to the black garden.

Don't worry about the mess,
the dustpan and brush are beside the bin.

Can You Help Me?

Can you help me?
I get to you in your chair,
pillows scattered around
like you've shed them,
head sagging onto your chest.
Where am I, Cocker?
My poor Dad, I say
and explain I've brought you home
from hospital to this.

I help you up on the Zimmer.
My arm across your shoulder,
we lock heads like two props
in a scrum and I smell
your trickle filling the bowl.

Door open, I fall asleep
and wake to the wood pigeon's
three dry notes, thinking
it's you calling. Later,
I turn off the radio mid-sentence
and when brushing my teeth, stop.

Driving home, I want to pull over
in a quiet spot, wind down the windows
and check I can't hear you.

Like something lost, you've slipped
behind the rustle of the paper,
wind tugging the roof,
my tinnitus when I lie in bed.
Can you help me?

22

After Closing Time

It has to be after midnight
and too many Bacardi and Cokes to count;
Mum has to be in bed and Dad
not getting gyp from his gout,
not listing things that get on his tits.
That's when he tells me
how the stench in Chislet Colliery
was so thick from dust and men
that walking through cobwebs
wouldn't come close.

See, there were no toilets,
you'd just find a spot
or do it on your spade
and chuck it on the conveyor.
Then, to clear your airways,
you'd eat a whole onion,
chew it like an apple
to scour the grimy passages.

And if you were lucky
the coal would be good
and slip off the face,
sometimes leaving an entire fern
millions of years old.
The men would come round,
point their torches and look
before you drilled out the bastard
in the way of your bonus.

It's then I offer to get another drink
but my dad seems lost
like he's told me his last story
and there's nothing else to say.

Cocker

My dad called me Cocker
when I was young, not son.
I didn't want my friends
to hear him say it.
Then, for years, nothing.
But recently, kneeling
to pick up his legs
to swing them into the footwell,
the word's come back.
I start the engine.
He turns on the radio
loud, *Let's go, Cocker.*

Acts of Faith

I was at work when it happened –
work not *school* you'd always insisted,
seeing it was more than long holidays.
You were in your favourite chair,
looking out at the apple tree.
At first Mum couldn't get you
onto the floor to do the kiss of life
until the *very kind* ambulance crew
tried CPR for half an hour
to get you back. The Year Eights
had done a list of containers: a bag,
locket, fridge, coffin, I'd said
by way of examples – gospel. Then
we'd described what was inside each,
crossed out all the containers
and titled the piece 'Inside my Head.'
As a finale – the bell was due –
we all stood as we'd done before
and, after three, we read our thoughts
at the same time, to Jason,
the aspidistra, who was thriving
on the shelf above the dictionaries.
With his twenty green, alert ears,
he'd hear each individual voice
and wave if he was happy.
After the simultaneous cacophony,
we all had to go but Phillipa,
our TA, stopped me just to say –
the atmosphere, they were all reading,
rapt, facing the plant – like a choir.

Morphic Resonance
(For Sean)

Walking with Craney in Langdale,
we talk about Herdwicks, as you do,
and about morphic resonance. Apparently,
in sodden Wales, the outback
and the Andes where it never rains,

they're trotting up to cattle grids,
cocking their heads and chewing
over why their limbs are so sticky.
Then the sheep lie on their sides
and, like barrels, roll over the bars.

Once the sky stops spinning,
they kick out their back legs
and gambol away like lambs.
That would be that, except later
you're leading the last pitch:

the bag of your bum and legs
and flailing arms gone
above the buttress. I'm belaying
while taking a pee, trying not
to swap my hands. Thud.

A sheep lands beside me
with a grunt. Stone dead.
Maybe it had cocked its head
and out-thought its legs. Later,
at the top of Harrison Stickle,

we chew it all over and picture
sheep across the world teetering
on the edge, bouncing into the air
to be clouds and me found dead
beside a black one, willy out.

Showering on a Campsite

Go before or after. Pray
for a hook behind the door
or a six-inch nail. Attempt
the blurry, Biro instructions.
Inspect the lock. Rattle it.
In advance, stack your change
on the meter. Strip like
you're on a promise: socks
in shoes, pants in pocket.
Under the naked bulb,
forget flexing your pecs.

Go for it. Slam in
a 20. Heaven is warmth –
that glove of pleasure – but
expect third-degree burns
or Chinese drip torture.
Cries only bring toddlers
counting legs. Ignore
blue tiles of windmills,
the abyss of the plughole. Soap
dropped is soap lost.
Dream of a slate wet room.

Wash top down: hair,
pits, smelly bits; the farmer
will have fixed time.
Avoid clingy boxers
by double-handed towelling
like working a two-person saw.
Aspire to friction burns.
Bounce around on a foot.
Sling your tropical towel
over your shoulder matador-style.
Step into Wensleydale rain.

The Truth about Gaffer Tape

Keep your duck, artist and spike –
give me gaffer tape: a sexy black
and smooth as a freshly shaved back.

Waterproof, you stick for England. Look,
there's a patch on my walking trousers
holed by my crampons. Oh my square limpet.

Vinyl-coated cotton gauze, you're ideal
under the government's efficiency savings
for eyepatches, broken limbs and slings.

Your journey from humble adjective to verb
is conjugated in schools: to gaffer, gaffers,
gaffering. Your future, an adverb of time.

When you've got a gangster or your boss
tied to a chair in a disused warehouse
and he won't leave it alone, you're perfect.

Ah gaffer tape, sole of my shoe,
invented by NASA with space blankets,
Speedos and infrared ear thermometers.

A chunky roll around the neck
wards off evil spirits. You're all that's needed
on a desert island apart from a pig.

Called a hundred miles an hour tape
by Nam helicopter vets, Michelangelo
dreamed of you for his marble amputees.

In the park, the runners have gaffered up
their nipples and private parts. And the lovers
share a reel for their broken hearts.

My Life in Contraceptives

None at first. We started with tickling,
ended counting off days. Then condoms.
As nervy about Fruit Cocktail Flavour
as buying you that G-string, the size
of an eyepatch and half as attractive.

Once I tried on a Deluxe Durex
and glowed in the dark. A mate shrugged:
you didn't eat a Mars in the wrapper.
Your doc put you on the pill, shedfuls.
No mention of side effects or the Big C.

I pictured a time as wild as buying
The Joy of Sex with those sketches of a guy
in nothing except his beard but settled for
watering the back yard with the hose.
Those sweet days of sin before kids.

Now, an economy pack with the shopping.
The cap? Strictly for the shower. The coil?
Like making love to a wire brush.
Next, the knacker's yard with the dog.
I'm more excited by the weather forecast.

You sit down to tell me some news:
Somehow, I think I'm pregnant. Although
my eyes are tea bags, my stubble grey,
I say, *All my sperm drive tanks.*
You stare, *Still Jack the fucking Lad.*

31

Middle Age

Ah those catalogues of Christmas gifts:
shoehorns, ear-hair trimmers, luxury
tweezers, periscopes for looking at your back.

You doze off at 4am to the History Channel,
the siege of Stalingrad, dreaming your children
have nothing to eat except wallpaper paste.

They leave home to live far away. Always
you cook too much for tea. That's you
standing in their rooms dusting their photos.

You dare not calculate when you'll retire:
it's jam tomorrow or jam tomorrow.
In the Sunday papers, you can sail the Aegean.

You'd drop out if there was somewhere to drop to.
The Youth Hostels are packed with students
and the greys. At least you still hate golf.

You take up jogging, running, marathons,
could recite Personal Bests if anyone
would listen. Your Lycra is top of the range.

Varnished with sweat, you shout at dogs.
Blondie's on your iPod. Lit from behind,
she's ahead at the pouting fork in the road.

You've rehearsed excuses for dinner parties,
not tempted by wine cellars, swingers
or their bubbly daughter just back from Oz.

You love your wife and not out of habit:
she's stood a lifetime of winters on the touchline,
cheering on your sons and doing the teas.

You don't fancy your secretary but notice
what she's wearing. Sex gnaws away.
Missionaries try more positions. You eye

the kitchen table, stairs, the back
of the Skoda but the upholstery's beige.
Your wrist aches more than a teenager's.

Tips

Get closer to the ground. Hack
the legs off your career ladder.
Sneak into your boss's PowerPoint
a slide titled Early Austrian Orchids.
Learn the names of trees.

Trespass across Private Land.
How can you own a stream?
Steal a little red scooter and zip
through your local skatepark
pushing away kids in the face.

Buy a boa constrictor to coil
around your naked chest
and when the neighbour asks
about its poodle-shaped lump,
tug your bottom lip.

Go commando and feel your bits
flop about like a just-landed cod.
Never send Christmas presents;
buy your sister a goat in Gambia
and give it her name. Be happy

hating dogs. Regrow down there.
Run ice cubes over the topography
of your loved one. Perfect feigning
fits. You're dying inside out.
Wonder why there's water on the Earth.

Practise five ways to knot a rope
and make sure you need them.
Know different words for home.
Find the world to run in,
your skeleton gleaming like chrome.

Between the Game and Chaos

Your 10p spins in the air,
catches the sun, Theatre of Dreams,
but don't let it hit the ground.
8 and 4 will be bickering about
the angle it's stuck in the mud.

Rings and piercings – that can
be seen – must be removed.
Remember every call riles someone.
Next, the match ball. Spherical.
The pressure? At sea level.

This little fella's your friend:
my Super II whistle knocks out
fifty decibels. Now, the caution,
longer and louder – Blue 10,
you did, a word in your conch-like.

Penalty? Watch out for the Suárez,
the Big Mac and Fries. Yellow it.
But if it isn't and it is, it is.
Don't get mullahed yourself, bang –
red him, see ya later, sunshine.

Don't be wishy-washy. Think
Collina with his marble eyes,
think Cloughie, *You're doing greatly
and will never be with the timid
fearing defeat.* The life of Brian.

The end of the game? In reality,
your time is the only time.
Point at the centre. Quality.
Hit two massive pips, then
the trilly bit, like this.

I Met Mick McManus

(i.m. Mick McManus)

A wicker basket of primroses,
rouged cheeks, smile:
I was studying a figurine
in the long display cabinet
as he explained the Bow factory
was close to the slaughterhouses.
Bone for bone china.

But all I could think about
was my nan shouting at the TV
that McManus was a dirty cheat;
the same man saying Canton
was warm and creamy like ivory.
And that, he pointed, *was our first;*
Barbara bought it for my birthday.

I glanced at his glass reflection.
As he gathered himself,
I saw again the black hair
and eyes, the two cauliflowers
that made the Dulwich Destroyer
plead to Jackie Pallo, *Not*
the ears, not the ears.

Instead of asking about
the capsules of pig's blood,
I thought of Nan. After
she died, I heard my grandad
smacked her round the room,
wall to wall to wall.
The man you loved to hate.

When I started listening again,
Mick was talking about resonance,
strength, whiteness, translucency:
Look. Opening the door,
he reached in for a plate
and, holding it up, I could see
the perfect outline of his hand.

Ana Mladić Remembers Her Father

My first memory of him, at the end of the garden,
face dark behind a veil, body robed in smoke
to disarm the hives, lulling them into a calm.

Once he popped some propolis into my mouth
for a sore throat while I painted Tutankhamun
asleep in his tomb, next to a pot of honey.

Later he schooled me in queens and drones
as he scooped out the light from honeycombs,
fretting about Colony Collapse Disorder.

When he graduated, Father was awarded
a pistol, his favourite. I promised to fire it
on the day the next in the Mladić line was born.

That last time I returned, he met the bus,
patted my cheek, brought me sweets,
his little *Chetnik* cap above his big face.

I'd seen the war on TV in Moscow, asked
if he'd ordered all Muslim signs to be burned.
He laughed, *Allah can't help but Ratko can.*

I stared at him till he snapped, *The bees
from a single hive fly around the world
six times to yield one pound of beeswax.*

I knew then it was true. My father, my dad.
I chose his pistol. The coroner noted
a gun was an unusual weapon for a woman.

I imagine him at the Srebrenica memorial,
clutching a red rose, scanning the lists
and lists of the missing, not finding my name;

staggering up the garden through the smoke;
in his head, the dark hole of a mouth –
the hives silent and his bees all dead.

Storywaters

Looking for Warlawarru

Our first night in Cairns,
Tropical North Queensland.
Baggage dumped, kids
in the softness of sleep,
we sprawl across the veranda.

Basking in warmth,
we try reading the stars
for the eagle, Warlawarru,
and its nest, the Coalsack.
The sky's all mixed up.

Waxy greens rustle.
You fidget, blurt out
something to tell me:
I think I'm pregnant.

Something? Stars
fade. *Good,* I say.

You reach out, draw
me in, find a white limb
and make it my arm
around you.

My cheek. Your neck.
A kiss is kisses,
tongues of sweetness,
shedding our clothes,
leading each other
somewhere known as if
we can make tonight
the first night of life,
of conception.

A veranda in Cairns.
Rainforest circled around us.
Your untied hair
blonde on my bare chest.
Your finger joins the stars,
trying to find Warlawarru.

Test

You dunk the strip
like a school girl
with litmus paper.

Moisture creeps
to your fingerprints.
Your mouth twitches.

Seconds are grainy,
molecules of pink
haemorrhaging red.

A line is drawn.
Positive.
You risk a smile.

I push down
your arms around
my neck,

walk out,
the fuse burning
in your fingers.

Dream-spirit

That crouched lad
with a fist of cowries
is our George. And there,
Ashley skimming a stone.

What are we doing
holidaying in Port Douglas,
days tanned, beach
fringed with T-shirt palms?

If only we'd planned
our family, could sit
together opposite the doctor
who'd smile and begin.

Instead, we're shunting
bedrooms, calculating costs,
adding 20 years to 37
and imagining a life.

Four Mile Beach.
We've told no one, sit
like grandparents watching
their grandchildren swim.

Behind us, some kids
have found a goanna,
jewellery head to tail,
a dream-spirit dreaming.

Nothing

In the dead of night,
you ring our GP
back home: *Amnios*
– safe as houses.
You've nothing to lose.

Gritty hours to dawn.
Cystic fibrosis:
you name spiky words
to gamble with;
this speck of life
on its tight orbit.

Morning. Light sharpens.
On our Far Side calendar,
we tear off a day.
Time's stung itself.

You're fifteen weeks.
Twenty the red line
with nothingness beyond
perhaps for – it, dare
I say you, foetus,
baby, child.

Chance

I. Echuca

Before flying home, we'd travel
– that glitzy word – to Lake Mungo,
its craters of sand fished by clans
40,000 years ago. Moonscapes,
a perch cooked by Mungo Man
or Mungo Woman, now a fossil;
the midden trail once lapped
by the lake, kids splashing
in the shrieking water.

II. River Cruise

Our youth wasn't misspent.
Now we can't spend it, going bush.

The Emmylou paddles us along the Murray,
banks sherbet- yellow with wattles,
white with limbs of eucalypts.

Slumped in a chair, you shade
your eyes, try to rub away
sickness in your belly.

III. The Heritage Port

In Sharp's Arcade, one penny clinks
into Granny's Prophesies. She sings:
A trip round the world is in store,
Bringing more happiness than before.
Then a lucky number.

Stars shoot around her head.
Squaring up, my bloodshot eyes
stare back. We're through with plans,
give us the number: 401.

Playing God

The jittery line is not
a heartbeat on a monitor
but your signature
on the disclaimers.

Our family circles the bed.
Your belly's polished with gel.
DVD in – action.

What looks like a windscreen
on a wild Yorkshire night
with shapes looming out of the murk
is the scan of our baby
with the moon for a skull.

Ashley hopes for kicks,
turns – breaststroke;
our George, a widge, a mate
to play for Arsenal too.

But the doctor pronounces you
on the downhill side of 14,
not the 15 weeks prescribed:
With an amniocentesis,
we don't play God.

We're shown the door,
clutching DVD, photo
and appointment card for
the day before our flight
to the edge of Europe.
Days are few, feel
easy to break.

Fitzroy Gardens, colours
bleached. A ghost gum.
As the kids squabble,
we huddle together,
sharing the close-up:
a hand of white pebbles,
fingers of chalk –
hello and goodbye.

Amniocentesis

As the receptionist studies
our insurance details,
the gynaecologist appears
from behind a curtain;
needle long and thick.

I stroke your arm.
The syringe angles into
the sponge of womb,
pierces the wet image,
feet webbed in shadow.

She interlocks her fingers
and turns her palms inside
out to click her knuckles.
Gripping the plunger,
she sucks out cloudiness,
holds it to the light.

After, she scans you,
trying to pull an image
from the swirling grey.
Glimpses of limbs slide away.
There, isn't he delicate?

So, a boy? Our boy
in there where the tide's out.

OK? she asks
moving to the machine,
our son slipping
off the screen.

Departures

I close the curtains on
our rope hammock sagging
between the olive trees.
A kookaburra laughs
manically in drizzle.

Over tea, next door,
we chat away the last hour:
beach weekends at Lorne,
southern right whales
calving off Logan's Beach
for thousands of years,
nuzzling into each other.

Minutes fall. Our stories
will keep us neighbours.
The airport shuttle bus
steps up the gears.
Friends fade to outline.

Flying over the outback,
maybe a goanna turns
its head to the plane's drone.
We wonder where we're going,
going home.

47

Gone midnight, we ring
and ring and ring
the wooden bungalow,
the surgery on Sturt.

A musical hello
becomes a fact – names,
dates, Dawson Street South –
pops us on hold.

Hisses from the line. Then
her voice smoothes out crackles:
*Yes, everything's good;
the number's normal.*

I brew some tea
for something to do,
rinse the pot imagining
a doctor flushing your cells –
each of 46, 46, 46 –
down the sink, down
into the Southern Ocean.

Weeks later, as you soak
in the bath, a sparrow
sings on the window sill,
sings, as for the first time,
our baby kicks out ripples.

Nursery

The study has to go, my
study with 70s roses,
blistered gloss and damp
leaching the chimney breast.
My garden shed, smelling
of dusty books and me.

A bubble of pine sap
from Thunder Bay, my fossil
of a cockle shell, small
as a pea, bagged, boxed.

Empty, sounds bounce.
These last days:
the pendulum of the brush.

The finishing touch:
a clip-framed watercolour
of a mob of kangaroos
painted by your mum.

The cot's instructions
baffle an afternoon until
it's perfect. Your room's
done. The first thing
I've done for you.

Now to rest, imagine
your vanilla scent,
mustard stools,
your wobbling face.
Alive and so light,
you filling this space.

First Contact

No time for words,
I just hum for you,
resting my cheek
on the tight drum
of your mum's stomach.

Her belly button
is inside out,
the knot of the balloon
in which you float,
a naked astronaut.

The song of your heart.
Your mum's double bass.
Then a new pattern,
making three, life
from another universe, me.

Ghost Ward

Afternoon's empty.
The high bed. You whiter
than your white gown.

The incision from hip to hip
will leave a scar like a smile,
Dr Choudry notes.
You sign, consent to surgery.

We swap names for a son,
weigh the colour of each
syllable until it loses shape.
You feel our child turn
over, nestle against
the cot of the rib cage.

In a stack of magazines,
you find a feature
about the Dreamtime.
We gaze into the Coalsack
again, the grainy nebula.

Your finger joins stars
of the Southern Cross
that's also the Eagle's Foot,
Warlawarru. One's the other.

Time's void. The doctor
will restart it at 7pm
when our son's sky will be
sliced and light born,
our ghost take form.

Washing Up

The anaesthetist smiles:
You'll only feel like
someone's washing up
inside your stomach.

She shoots morphine
into your *lovely spine,*
strokes your cheeks
and calls your name
from the rim of darkness.

This time, no stirrups,
bedpans, bastard swearing,
you thrashing like a fish
held down in air.

At 7.13, the magician
reaches in to lift out
life. Our baby's gripped
by his heels and bleats
as he's weighed.

Womb-curved, slimy,
floating in my arms,
a boy, a son, our son.
You little bugger, you say.

On his breathing skin,
creams, blood
and my purged fears
shed as tears.

Warlawarru

I drive our children
to meet their brother,
thinking of my wife:
baby cut out,
the empty skin,
Storywaters gone.

Standing in a circle,
Ashley blurts out:
He's red – as a plum,
like he's been cooked.

A water-fine smudge
of blond hair,
pink shells for nails,
each finger printed
with its ripples.

You, our Storywaters:
goanna, sparrow,
your hand's hello,
molecules of red dye,
Warlawarru in the sky,
our lucky number 401,
it, foetus, he, our son.

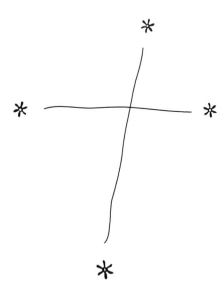

Knee Music

All washed up on the sofa –
ice cream bowls, wrappers,
legs across the coffee table.
James Bond has just saved
the known world when Jack
says out of the blue, *Look*
and by tensing his quads,
his knees move. *Guess
the song,* he says. Oddly,
we fail to get *Hard Sun.*
The dimply circles drum
and we're in bits when
his sister shouts correctly,
We Will Rock You.
Eyes down, we're off again
to one kneecap pulsing,
run through the discography
of Queen, Abba, Shamus Dark,
Adele. Finally we give in.
Jack grins, *It's the heart.*

Sledging
(All Saints' Field)

We eye up the gateposts, stack the sledge,
oldest and heaviest at the back; more arms
and legs than a beetle. Weight and gravity
grab us. Slush and mud and grass

spatter our faces. Screams when a dip
throws our stomachs in the air. Of course
it ends in carnage: bodies and hats
strewn, mangled. We are never cold.

We go again and again, fill the afternoon.
Sometimes we abort: a dozy man
with a dozy dog, a toddler spinning
around, a jogger in next to nothing.

Snow ices over – polystyrene. A train
floats across fields, the petrol station
turns into a spaceship and there,
the snowball of the moon stuck on the sky.

Chips off the old block, we wedge ourselves in,
stare out the two pillars. Our laughter's
our slipstream. Within touching distance,
we scrape our sledge along some rocks.

Beached on rubble, we fall out sideways,
panting. Our hair's wet with snow.
We pull each other up and turn together
to give the impossible just one more go.

The End of George's Last Football Season

George, I see you lounging on the sofa,
playing Fifa with your little brother;
the banter about offsides. You're all pecs
and torque. We don't wrestle any more,
your grip is steel and you always win.

It's time for you to leave home
while you still know everything. I won't
miss your shrugs or the used plasters
and pulped towels on your bedroom floor.
In six short months, I've become my dad.

No wild camping in Moidart, stomping
past manes of ice up Window Gully
to top out in sunset's peachy glow;
you're jetting to Zante with Tommy G
and Dirt Box for a foam disco.

But that's us pegging out the nets
on Sunday morning for over 10 years,
shovelling dogs' mess off the pitch, me
flagging offside, as a ref being abused
by the other manager. A knob-jockey.

That's us replaying highlights in slow mo,
car full of your gappy smile: Harrogate
where you bossed midfield, Catterick –
a smash and grab and the seconds dying,
Nelson where you slipped a ball

through into another dimension. Tonight
as I drive out of town, every rec
is haunted by a dad watching his son.
Pitches fall dark, white lines fade.
A goal left up, leaning to one side.

The Furthest Yellow Buoy

This poem isn't about anything,
just the beach at Deauville,
the cries and surf in French.

We've played the weather:
sun with a sarong of cloud
stops our legs burning.
Paddling up to our knees,
we throw the sopping ball
to explode in our hands.

You fancy a swim, eye
the furthest yellow buoy.
Your mum would sigh
at such manliness.
We leave your brothers
knocking each other over,
diving like keepers.
In the cradle of each wave,
we put in our breaststroke.

Resting, we bob up
and down on our backs,
toes out, gondola-style.
A lifeguard in his powerboat
sniffs around for a rescue.
We giggle at what to say,
what's *messing about*?

Beneath us, that bulk
of heaviness as I quiz you
about your gap year:
Tanzania, Australia,
a flat round the corner.

On your shoulder, I let you
touch the buoy first,
a flask of fibreglass smudged
with green, spattered by gulls.
Angry wet bikes rip past.

We kick off in the rhythm
of each other. The sea
lifts us as it breathes.

Returning is shorter.
The thin line of yellow
grows fat. A breeze
catches tinny sounds.

We lurch up the sand. I grab
a towel for your shoulders
as an excuse to hug you,
to squeeze warmth in.
This poem is about everything:
my daughter, my Ashley.

Jack and the 3G

Seven steps back, two to the left,
legs apart, deep breath –
you'd studied Ronaldo on YouTube.

3G is the new grass,
though later it'll be me picking up
black rubber bits from the carpet.
You diss the tarmacked playground
I used with your brother, then blast
the free kick into the car park.

Under the eye of the clock tower,
you try a double elastic
in your AC Milan shirt
with gold lettering, me in a cagoule,
bobble hat and gloves, jeans
tucked in for a sporty look.

These days, I don't do the commentary
but shout the odd headline:
scorcher, dipper, curved like a banana.
Next year, you'll be a teenager
going to town with your mates.

A shower drags through,
trashes seagulls and pins litter
to the fence. We keep on.
Throw-ins: feet and back,
give and go, the lob into the box.

Eight thirty, Sunday morning,
toasty to the core, the only
people on the whole 3G,
the only ones in the world.
Penalty shoot-out to come.

Steps

Even though you've left home
and probably don't remember,
I can't take the two steps down
to the back door – the stone steps
I set in concrete one summer
and called you to leave your handprint –
without seeing you sprinting
in your dress, white shoes,
blonde hair full of speed,
me thinking the steps and your legs
would miss each other and you falling,
falling through the years to smack
your forehead again on the bluntness
of the doorstep and always, too late,
me running towards you.

Note

They met at college.
She'd piercings at the top of her ear.
That time down by the lake,
she'd touched his scar,
her fingers described its shape:
a longboat with oars.

At Symonds Yat,
eased down the cliff,
she'd thrown her hands wide
but he'd gripped the harness.

Then the twins came along.
He'd take them to the park,
kneel to watch the sparrows.

After the girls went to bed,
she'd follow, exhausted,
leaving him alone
with his OU degree.

When the girls were teenagers
on sleepovers or out partying,
she sat under the lamp.
Sometimes on the way home,
he'd stop at the reservoir car park.

He waited till the girls had gone,
were doing nicely, everything
was doing nicely. He remembered
Gaping Gill: one Bank Holiday
he'd declined being lowered
into the dark, though she was keen.

You'd hardly know it was there,
that empty cavern
big enough to hold St Paul's.

It was a normal week day.
He left his briefcase at the top.
The police said he left no note.

Notes for a Successful Affair

Delete your mobile's Call History.
Don't start buying silk boxers or skinny
ties. Find the time: golf's perfect
as you choose the number of holes.
Invent some friends and give them problems
their wives wouldn't begin to understand.

Avoid whistling a tune from The Charts;
peck your other half on the cheek.
Rehearse your reasons: you wouldn't mind
if your beloved had a dalliance with
a Danish waiter in Berlin. A city break.
It might set fire to your dead bed.

The law of nature says look at anything –
except swans. In any affair, there's one
consenting woman. Guilt is dishonesty
of motive. Anyway, what does it matter:
the hotel's booked. Rooms by the hour,
all day – you can slip away for lunch.

And she does that little thing with her tongue,
says, *So, what are you going to do
about it?* Only you can make her purr.
You're stripped to the wire. The sheets are clean.
If it wasn't for this affair, you'd have left
your wife years ago. You're doing it for her.

Accidental Death

She bought a new double bed
and paid to have the living room
redecorated in the magnolia she'd wanted
all along. If you're wondering
did she sit up in bed at night
dreaming she could see his body
rising from the dark under the ice,
his face calm like he was young,
she didn't. He was a serious man,
so only an average number attended.
The vicar hadn't met him personally.
He still had his GPS. in his pocket
when they found him, so he knew
exactly where he was. His hair
and eyelashes were crystal white.
A girl the age of his daughter
found him washed up on the shore.
No one was certain but an ex-teacher
had seen someone like him
on the summit of Helvellyn the day before.
His car was covered in plumes
of ice. They'd rubbed a hole
to see if anyone was still inside.
The car was located at the back
of a pub close to the lake.
The police knocked at their door.

Swimming with Jellyfish

For fun, the dolphins race the prow,
flip their white bellies over
for the crowd, some of whom run

from one side to the other. Even
his wife smiles, gripping the rail.
After, she drives them up the coast.

The balcony of their flat seems suspended
in the sea fret. She goes to lie down.
On the beach, sun presses to get through.

Families have parasols. Kids are netting
jellyfish: in a dinghy full of water,
they are pulsing like hearts, red

on yellow plastic. Wanting to be stung,
he swims into coolness. His fingers flinch
as he brushes them but he pushes on.

He thinks gentle breaststroke might save him –
a jellyfish drifts through his arms, kisses
his cheek. He splashes as if his feet

are tangled but no one can see him.
The ocean grows darker feeding on
the pale mist. Trawling a wake behind,

he makes the beach. The kids have vanished.
Jellyfish on sand, their buoyancy and gloss,
a gritty blob. Too late for them.

In the mirror, his face stares back.
On the raised skin, a red line,
an incision, tingling like an electric shock.

His wife gets antiseptic, cleans and cleans it,
doesn't ask why, rests her fingertips
on the exact place he'd been stung.

Blind

It's as if I'm invisible, he said
as they stood in the kitchen.
They didn't shout any more, it was like
they were discussing a lamp shade
for the living room. She cried
a few tears. It made no difference.
When he was washing up, she didn't
put her arms around his belly
and her cheek flat to his back.

He grew a beard as she never kissed him.
Then that time in the spare bedroom.
He stared out at the terrace opposite:
bats – the miracle of their flight.
The room filled with darkness,
constellations finding their place,
when she bustled in with the washing,
switching on the light
so all the stars went blind.

Listen

If you leave our children playing in the garden
with their grandma, stroll down the shady drive,
follow the path between the oaks, their branches
lagged with moss. You'll find the stream.
You can't miss it there, gathering sunlight.

Go through the iron kissing-gate unattached
to any wall and let the stream lead you
towards its source. There'll be water-plantain
and yellow irises where cows come down to drink.
Ignore the wooden bench with its plaque.

Beyond tall shadows where the path
swerves in from the bank, an ash overhangs
a pool. Take off your shoes on the grass.
There are boulders as smooth as you want,
one to sit on, another for your back.

Ripples will play with the underside of leaves.
A few flies. Fish nudging the surface. There
a wagtail, bobbing about. That's where I'll be,
perhaps writing this or watching the trees
calm down the wind. Take my hand.

We'll paddle, wade in only as far
as you want, let the air dry our feet,
sun lift our footprints from the stones
as the stream tells its story to the sea. Set off
before it's dark. It isn't far. Come soon.

Frisbee

A frisbee is a miracle, spinning
backwards to fly forwards.

Thrown, it interprets the air,
veering round knots of wind

or keeps low to rise
like a tee shot with a driver.

Some days the best place
to be is the park with others.

You, my love, throw backhand,
often forgetting to let go.

I'm all swanky forehand
like I'm skipping a stone.

You could call it a game.
Then one leaves my grip:

I know it will fly straight
and true as if by radar.

You open your palm and take
the yellow frisbee out of the sky.

There it is above your head
and that's you shouting, *Yes*.

Diving on Tongue Reef

Remember the coral sea,
sea of language.

Remember the fluttering
shoals switching themselves on
and off in sunlight. Clown,
angel, trumpet and butterfly all making sense
with fish. And those beyond
words that just are, their squibs
and spangles arousing vision.

Remember warmth lapping
over our backs. Gardens
of pineapples and brains
mixing metaphors. Leaves
of gold around our heads.

Remember the stony lump,
stiff legs flicking, nosing
over reef and reef, the turtle
needing a verb of its own.

We follow, hand in hand,
slip free of weight.
Between a liquid sky
and the flowers of the sea,
we fly.